When I was asked to write a children's book about the Milk Bank, I was excited to be able to honor our donors in such a special way. I feel privileged to have served on the Founding Board of the Mid-Atlantic Mothers' Milk Bank and count those 6 years as a true highlight in my 4 decade career. All proceeds from the sale of this book will be my personal "donation" to the Mid-Atlantic Mothers' Milk Bank.

Jan S Mallak, 2LAS, AdvCD-BDT(DONA)

To Denise O'Connor, founder and executive director of the Mid-Atlantic Mothers' Milk Bank, for having the vision to establish a Milk Bank in Pittsburgh so generous donors could provide their precious breastmilk to improve the health and well-being of medically fragile infants.

www.mascotbooks.com

An Ounce of Sharing... At the Milk Bank

For more information, please contact:

Mascot Books

620 Herndon Parkway, Suite 320

Herndon, VA 20170

info@mascotbooks.com

Library of Congress Control Number: 2019904261

CPSIA Code: PRT0819A

ISBN-13: 978-1-64307-326-2

Printed in the United States

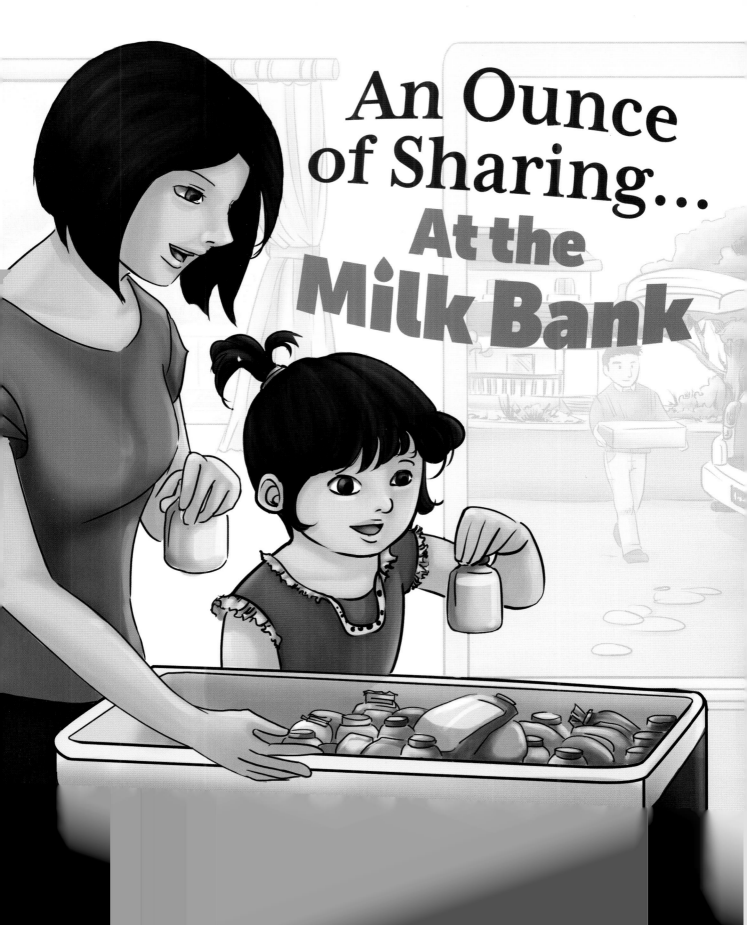

An Ounce of Sharing...
At the Milk Bank

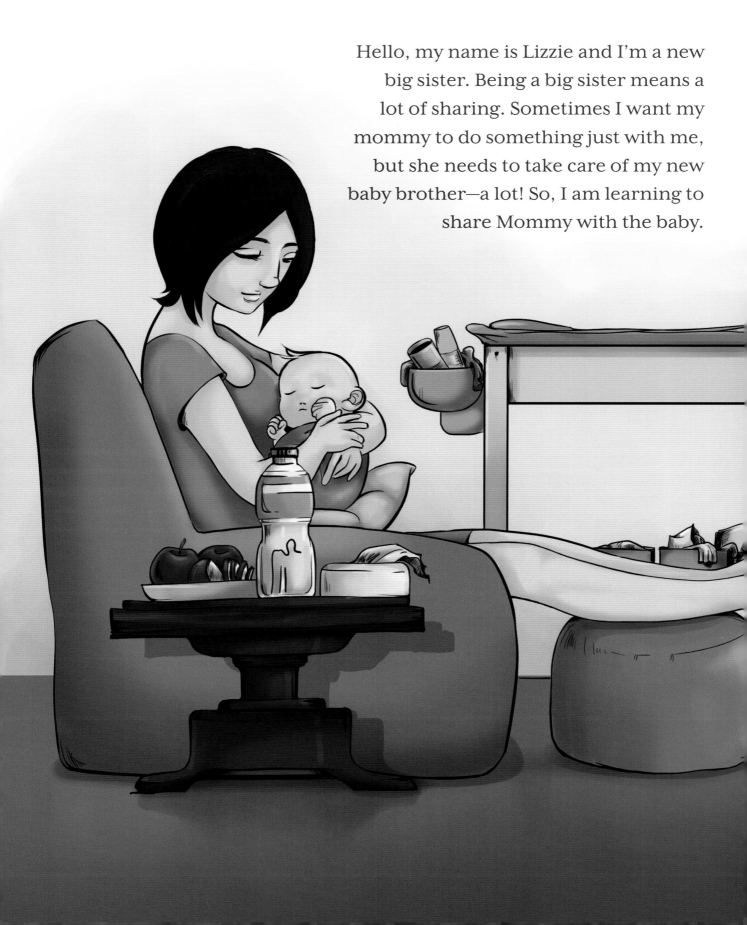

Hello, my name is Lizzie and I'm a new big sister. Being a big sister means a lot of sharing. Sometimes I want my mommy to do something just with me, but she needs to take care of my new baby brother—a lot! So, I am learning to share Mommy with the baby.

When the baby is breastfeeding, I like to talk to Mommy while I play with my puzzles. They are my favorite! Mommy tells me about how she also nursed me when I was a baby. Her milk made me healthy and strong, and it'll make my new baby brother healthy and strong too!

Mommy told me that some mommies can't breastfeed their own babies or make enough milk for them at first. Some babies are born too soon and are very tiny. Other babies are sick and breastmilk is like medicine for them.

When a baby has milk from another mommy it is called donor milk. Mommy says "donate" is a fancy word for share. Mommy wants to donate some of her milk today at the Milk Bank to help tiny and sick babies, and I get to go along! It feels good to know that we'll be helping other families.

The Milk Bank is a special place that collects donor milk and sends it to hospitals and homes for babies who need help. Mommy lets me help her pack up the frozen milk in a cooler to take to the Milk Bank. I can't wait for our tour of the Milk Bank!

We are ready to start our tour! The workers at the Milk Bank are called staff. They show us a classroom, a lab, and freezers full of milk.

They even have toys for kids to play with like my favorite, puzzles! Mommy especially likes the way it is decorated, and Daddy likes how neat and clean everything is. I am excited to see it all!

The nurse on staff tells us that before a mommy can donate milk, she has to answer some questions, have a test done, and get the doctor's okay. That helps make sure everyone is healthy. Mommy said it's easy to do and the Milk Bank pays for everything. That's so nice!

WELCOME TO THE MILK BANK

Families can either drop off the donated milk like we are doing or they can mail it right to the Milk Bank. There are even special boxes that can be used to keep the milk frozen. Wow, that's cool!

They have lots of freezers to store the frozen milk. The staff shows us milk that has just arrived. Some of it looks white, some of it looks yellow, and some milk even looks light blue. The staff explains that every mommy's milk is different, just like every child! I wonder what color my mommy's milk will look like next to other mommies' shared milk.

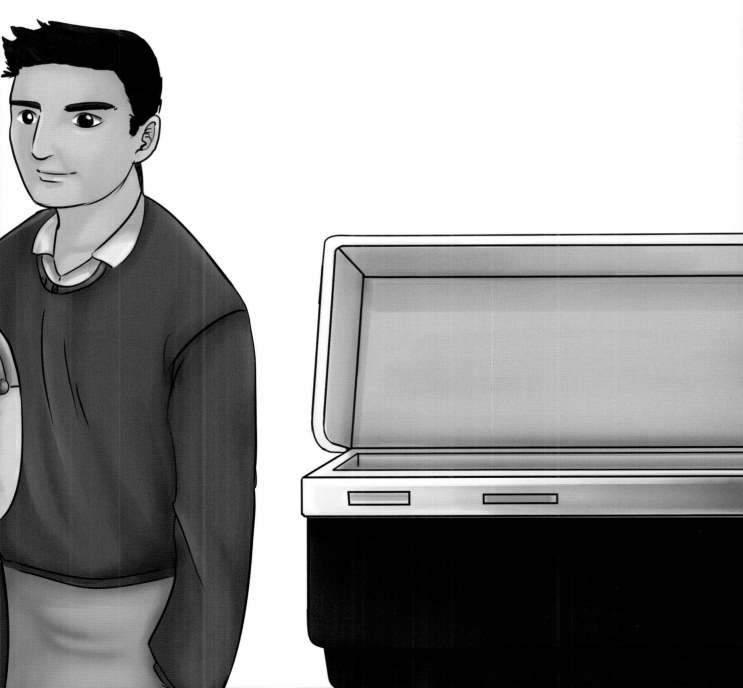

Milk from different mommies is thawed and put in bottles.
Then the staff puts the bottles into a special machine that
makes the milk safe for tiny and sick babies.

Next, the milk is sent to babies who need help to get stronger. Daddy says there is a special place in the hospital called a NICU. It's where the tiny and sick babies stay. They get extra care and are given breastmilk to help them grow and get better faster.

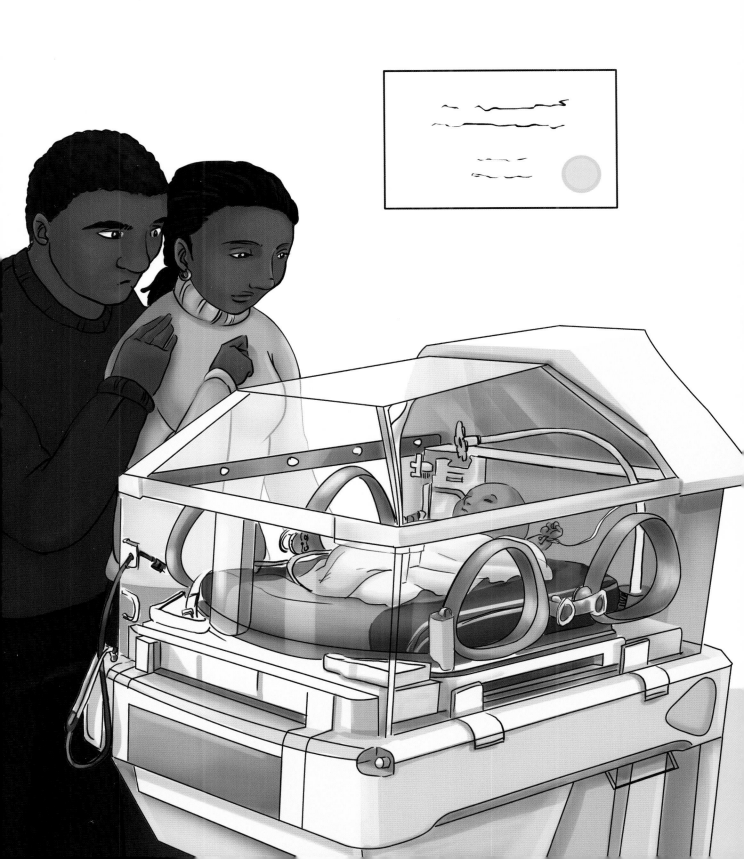

If babies need donor milk, a parent or nurse will feed it to them until their mommy is able to breastfeed. There are even special people at the hospital who can help mommies breastfeed their babies.

The parents, grandparents, doctors, and nurses are very happy when they see a tiny or sick baby grow because of the breastmilk.

They also like it when families do Kangaroo Care with their babies. Isn't that a funny name? It means that the baby is cuddled skin to skin with their mommy to make them feel warm and safe. That's how kangaroos take care of their babies. That sounds nice!

I think it's great that babies can get better because of the milk my mommy and other mommies donate until the babies' mommies can nurse the newborns themselves.

As our tour comes to an end, the Milk Bank staff says an "ounce of sharing" helps lots of babies and families. I'm so glad we can be a part of that ounce of sharing!

For the Grown Ups: About Milk Banks

Non-profit Milk Banks exist to improve health outcomes and to support breastfeeding. The majority of donor milk is used by infants cared for in neonatal intensive care units (NICUs). For a variety of reasons, many mothers with a baby being cared for in the NICU are unable to provide all of the milk that their baby needs, at least initially.

The use of donor milk for medically necessary supplementation in the NICU is associated with less complications, fewer infections, shorter hospital stays, and increased rates of maternal breastfeeding success. For these babies, human milk is truly lifesaving medicine.

Outpatient children with certain medical issues benefit from donor milk too.

Milk Banks that are part of the Human Milk Banking Association of North America (HMBANA) follow strict guidelines to ensure the safety of donor milk.

Donors are healthy mothers who make milk beyond the needs of their own baby. Sometimes, donors are bereaved mothers. All donors go through a screening process that includes a phone interview, statements from the healthcare providers of the donor and her baby, a medical history form, and blood screening. Donors are uncompensated volunteers. All screening and shipping costs are paid for by the Milk Bank.

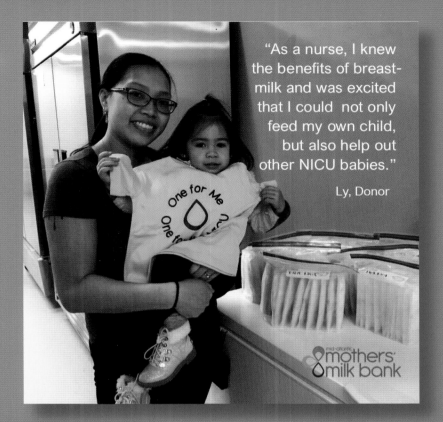

"As a nurse, I knew the benefits of breast-milk and was excited that I could not only feed my own child, but also help out other NICU babies."

Ly, Donor

Milk arrives to the Milk Bank frozen in bags or bottles. Prior to processing, the milk is thawed in a refrigerator. The thawed milk of up to five donors is pooled, mixed, and bottled.

The bottles are placed in water bath pasteurizing units. All HMBANA Milk Banks use a low temperature pasteurization method that eliminates pathogens while maintaining as much bioactivity as possible.

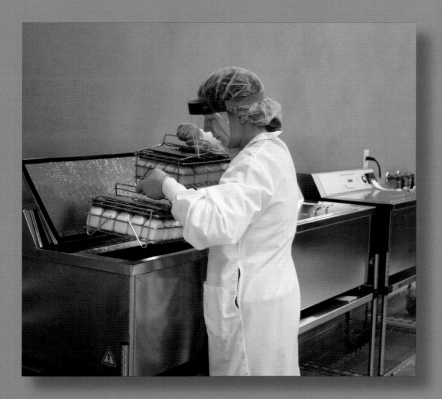

After pasteurization is complete, the bottles are cooled and labeled. Processed milk is stored frozen. A random bottle from each batch is sent to a lab for bacterial culturing. Milk may also undergo other testing such as nutritional analysis and drug testing.

"Our daughter has benefited greatly from donor breast milk supplied from our local Milk Bank, Mid-Atlantic Mother's Milk Bank in Pittsburgh, PA. Chloe was born prematurely with a congenital heart defect called hypoplastic left heart syndrome. After two surgeries, she was finally able to go home at 4 ½ months. Donor milk reduced her risk of life-threatening intestinal complications that are common in heart babies and provided her with infection fighting antibodies. Although she has a long journey ahead, she has overcome so much. Thank you to the donating mothers! You have made a great difference in Chloe's life!"

- Mom of Chloe, donor milk recipient

About the Author

Jan S. Mallak, 2LAS, AdvCD-BDT(DONA), has been in the "baby business" for almost 40 years. In that time, she has been a childbirth educator, birth/postpartum doula, doula trainer/mentor, doula service founder/executive director, birth consultant, volunteer, and author. Jan's book entitled *Doulas' Guide to Birthing Your Way* was published in 2010. When asked to write a children's book about the Mid-Atlantic Mothers' Milk Bank, Jan was up for the task.

Jan is a founding Milk Bank Board Member, first serving as the treasurer, and now as a general member/volunteer. She also established and facilitates the Milk Bank support group for bereaved families and brings her therapy dog for extra support. Jan feels privileged and honored to have been a part of the Milk Bank's initial vision and now its remarkable reality. Jan has been married to Frank for 47 years and could never have lasted in this career without his loving support. They have a married daughter (Heather and Dror) and one 10-year-old grandson named Zeev. They also have a son, Frank, Jr., who recently became engaged (to Donna who has three boys). As Jan gets closer to retirement, she knows how hard it will be to finally leave the Milk Bank and this wonderful career being in service to other women and their families.